To Oliv[...]

Stations
of the
Heart

Eddie Gibbons

With Best Wishes

Eddie
oct '99

THIRSTY
BOOKS

© Eddie Gibbons 1999

First published 1999
Thirsty Books
an imprint of
Argyll Publishing
Glendaruel
Argyll PA22 3AE
Scotland

The author has asserted his moral rights.

Acknowledgement and thanks are due to the editors of the following publications in which some of these poems first appeared: *Deliberately Thirsty, Scottish Book Collector, Cutting Teeth, Broken Fiddle, Leopard Magazine, Mica* and *Snakeskin*. Also to Stephen Mulrine and Jimmie MacGregor for broadcasting several of the poems on BBC Radio Scotland. And to the Scottish Book Trust for choosing the poem 'Out of Dates' as one of their 'Postcards for National Poetry Day 1999'

Thanks to Frank Habicht for kind permission to use his photograph 'Goodbye Sunshine' for the back cover. The photograph is from his book *in the sixties* (Axis Publishing 1 870845 30 7).

Cover Photograph © Corbis/Library of Congress

Subsidised by the Scottish Arts Council

THE SCOTTISH ARTS COUNCIL

British Library Cataloguing-in-Publication Data.
A catalogue record for this book is available from the British Library.
ISBN 1 902831 11 X

Printing
Bell & Bain Ltd, Glasgow

To my wife, Barbara; my daughter, Jennifer; my father, Ted.
and to the memory of my mother, Peggy.

'Don't worry, son.
One day your ship will come in.
– And you'll be at the railway station.'
                    Love from Mum and Dad xxx

                         (16th birthday card
                         message to the author)

Stations of the Heart

DREAMS & TRAIN SMOKE

Home and Away

as a
child
at home
in bed
he heard
stories
of
children
who
strayed
got
lost

were
found
dead

scared he
stayed
got
lost

at
home
instead

STATIONS of the *Heart*

A Liverpool Villanelle

A city has no boundaries.
It travels where its offspring roam.
My thoughts now shape what once shaped me.

Old clipper ships and slavery
are storylines in dusty tomes.
A city has no boundaries.

Twin talismans of heraldry
keep vigil on the Liver domes.
My thoughts now shape what once shaped me.

Black buildings grimed by industry,
where streets are streams of rusting chrome.
A city has no boundaries.

A boom-time town in '63,
as frothy as the Mersey foam.
My thoughts now shape what once shaped me.

Then shiny times, with poetry:
The Cavern's worldwide metronome.
A city has no boundaries.

Now Thatcher's plague-years legacy
has left it like some ransacked Rome.
My thoughts now shape what once shaped me.

My heart still beats, though distantly,
for that far place I still call home.
A city has no boundaries.
My thoughts now shape what once shaped me.

Consider the Lily

I dream of Aunty Lily
back in 1963,
prior to Larkin's ditty
and the Rutles' first LP.

She dated Paul McCartney
(or so she said to me)
but he never came for tea
in her flat in Wavertree.

She wore highheels and lippy
as red as St John's shirt.
She shaked the hippyhippy
in her minimini skirt.

Stomping in the Cavern,
twisting in The Sink,
gyrating in the Grafton
and posing in the Pink.

Lily smoked her Woodies
on long Locarno nights
and glimpses of her sussies
started many horny fights.

My darling Aunty Lily
was almost 23,
she gave me Wrigleys chewy
and let me watch TV.

I remember Lily:
so light, so flit, so flirt,
so feminine, so filly,
so frilly underskirt.

And I was small and happy
in 1963.
I loved my Aunty Lily
and Lily she loved me.

And It Was

Was a time inside my time I dwelled beneath the twin-bird towers. Many youths with voices came from the hollows underground. Women walked stiletto streets which shone when rain fell all around. And in the air were aeroplanes and on the sea were ships. Was a time that was my time when bright were eyes the long day down. When curvy girls in giggle clusters tripped the pulse and sang the heart. Was in the town that was my town and I was young upon the world. And my brother called me brother and my sisters shone with dreams. Friends I had with many faces and they upped me in my downs. Was a river city bred me. Buoyed me in my flood of years. My fears. Those crystal chandeliers. And all around were shops and houses. On the road were many buses. Hark! the Herald Angels sang. Come on you Reds! My father cried. And the ice cream van was holy and my granny tied the knot. Brightly shone the candled chapel. Father Son and Holy Smoke. In the room where childhood slumbered walls were four and future-facing. And the cup was on the saucer. In the grate a fire burned. Spooky Jesus smiled upon me and the walls were thick with saints. Bastards robbed my Granny's meter. Turned her over twice times three. God was in the television. Grandma had his autograph. Ninevahs were sung in school and minims chortled in the vespers. The car that knocked my sister over was a turquoise Kharman Ghia. Horror strips us down to heartbeats. All in horror naked are. Was a girl inside a poem ate the hearts of nightingales. And the poem was her coffin and the rain her lover's tears. Was a poem that's never ending. He the soldier. She the whore. She the matchstick-selling pauper. He the semen billionaire. And he gave until it hurt. Her. And the poet drew his pension. Drank himself to drink in verse. Comes the hour. Comes the moment. People in their stories walk. Legends rise like mist from pavements. Alchemised by psychic sex. And the smoke was in the chimney. And the rent was never paid. Fix the Pole star with your sextant. Box the compass. Spill the beans. Spill your semen into women. Fill them with the common gift. Come together in your seeding. Come together unto death. Come together in the void. The holy coma after sex. Everyone I knew in childhood placed a flower on my grave. I loved until my heart was bleeding. And I fucked the girl next door. Was in passion. Was in haste. Was in 1964. Come on you Reds! Come on you Reds! The Kop applauded when I came. And my father held my mother. And he whispered Love Me Do. And my tea was on the table. And he always shone our shoes. In our hearts glowed little candles. Filled us with an inner light. And a lifetime sped before us. Passed us by before we knew. And my mother died of fright. In the night. I was naked on the stairs when the midnight call came through.

Jesse James Joyce

The day's been as glum as a poet's accountant.
A little more adventure wouldn't go amiss,
so I'll saddle-up my poems and head 'em all out West . . .

I'll be The Lone Rhymer,
gunning for maverick metaphors
and vigilante verses
with silver-bullet six-shooters.
(Who was that masked muse?)

Or dressed up all in black atop a palamino,
catching Davy Crockett's hat
falling at the Alamo.

Poem,
Poem on the range . . .

Where desperado couplets
dressed in ponchos
and sombreros
pass out on tequilas
in El Paso haciendas.

I'll be Jesse James Joyce
with a Stevie Smith and Wesson
ambushing the Pony Express
for Seamus Heaney First Editions.

I'll pow-wow with Cochise
inside a ring of fire,

trading buffalo hides
for bows of burning gold
and arrows of desire.

Several boys named Sioux
will jostle for a view,
Sitting Bull will have to stand
to see above the crowd
as I read aloud
Custer's Last Stanza.

Then I'll scalp Andrew Motion
and become the first Poet Lariat.

A Winter's Mourning

And you were asleep
those paper-round mornings
I woke to chill air
and factory lights shining.

And always my father
was up before me,
waking the rooms
with his measured breathing.

And this was his duty,
his passion, his calling:
to kindle warm woods
in the cold of the hearth.

I sipped at my tea
as he biked off to work
and the house glowed with care
in the bitter blue dark.

Beneath urban stars
our lives were unfolding:
in council house stories
down subsidised streets.

This winter I'll visit
to kindle warm words
in the cold of his heart,
your memory's keep.

Platform Heels

A windowed wave, our last separation.
My heart's engine pounding with the train.
Moving away motion by motion,
out of the station, into the rain.

Missing you more instant by instant.
Were those tears, or the light playing tricks?
The sound of your heels in the distance,
like railway sleepers cooling in clicks.

Epilepigram for the Cisco Kid

The shock stopped
me in my tracks:
a plump old biddy
jammed and jazzed
to the floor,
poleaxed by a fit.

I thought it was
a form of
pavement-jiving
for the over-fifties.

An urban voodoo
working on the neurons:
her handbag reeling
like a football rattle,
her floral frock
jitter-bugging
in its electric twitch.

Jolting synapses
spun her spiderwise
into a shambles,
pinned like a bug
in its whirl.

Being The Kid,
I rode to the shops
to buy some caps
for my Colt 45
to put her out
of her misery.

When I got back
the woman had gone.

Kirkby Comanches
for sure,
I thought,

as I headed West
across the endless
redbrick praries
of Lancashire.

Spanners in the Works

'A workman is like a spanner
– when it's worn out you throw it away.'

A quote, circa 1969
fired within my earshot
by the owner of the factory
where I was then apprenticed
to five years erosion of the soul.

Old Bob Williams,
the implement in question,
due to retire that Autumn,
was to be sacked before Summer,
his eighty previous seasons
being spent in the Company
of that same Mr. Quote
upon whose name I spat.

Bob could tease the steel
to any shape he pleased.
He roved amongst dimensions
of ten thousandths of an inch.
He could strip mild steel to atoms
and dissect it into formulas.

His life was spent
nose against the grindstone,
where carborundum and tungsten
were wed in confetti sprays of sparks.

He was the great Methuselah
to us overalled apprentices.
The machine shop alchemist
who transmuted base metals
into aircraft, trains and cars.

Those days the teabreak papers
spoke of Moonshots, Woodstock and War.
Our conversation was more mundane
as a rule, but tongues were fuelled
by the attitude of Management
and discontent was rife amid the lathes.

An overheard word about the status
of the workers; tools disposable as spanners,
resounded louder than any Hendrix lick:
that prick, the fat cat with the Jaguar coupé
raised a hundred hackles with his arrogant retort
and stirred a nest of militants
at the bottom of the Class.

Every tradesman's gaze that day
was hard as hammers.
Sharp as sickles.

It Doesn't Happen Often

On the first of January 1961,
Korky the Cat
beamed from our Dandys,
urging us to turn the comic
upside down
and read the year:
(twist)
1961 . . . wow!!!
(twist)
1961 . . . cor!!!

Apparently
we'll have to wait
until the year
6009
for life
to impress us
once more.

Euston to Euclid

This journey
used to take forever.
The Guard informed me.

It still does.
I replied.

Passing the Tyne

The river today
is grey as Hammerite.
That half-sunken ship
is a lady's slipper
through which the fishes float.

A mile-wide meniscus
shims between the shores,
butterflied with Rorshach slicks,
sumptuous with rainbow oil.

Tall cranes wade
around Wallsend.
Huge reeds of jibs
jab the air with hooks.

Swan Hunter's
whistle launches
flotillas of souls
in overalled platoons
past hand-me-down children
in hand-to-mouth streets.

Down the town they meet.
in places thick with smoke
and accents,
where seven days' sweat
is poured into pints.

The city's other river
flows from glass to mouth;
pubs like shipwrecked
quinqueremes
harbour lounge-bar mariners
who steer unsteady courses
through unfathomed evenings.

Girl on a Train

There's a Northern aspect to her speech.
The Lilt on her lips whetting her tongue.
A third-finger ring, a book, a peach,
a fashion mag, a handbag unslung.

So easy to see the lure of trains;
this lazy appraisal of her mouth,
a journey around the curves and planes:
her North, Central and all stations South.

Graveyard Shift

The dream was going nowhere
until it dropped me at my work.
The car park was a constellation:
Vauxhall Astras, Ford Orions
and, of course, the Company hearse.

I clocked on at midnight and drifted
through to the coffee machine.
It hummed at an octave that
boiled the ears then spat out
a cupful of Café Noir.

The workshop was buzzing
on automatic, machines
read their codes and were
drilling and cutting.

ROV's, rudely yanked
from their sea beds,
slumped like drowned
dogs on the factory floor.

Their nametags looked sad
in the shadowy half-light:
Diablos and Demons
humbled by duty at
one thousand fathoms.

Upstairs in accounts
dark deals were unfolding.
Screens were scrolling
with profit and loss.
Payslips were printing
the wages of sin.

A fax came in from Doris Stokes.

The corridor lights
blipped on and off :
a cardiac decline
to that final flat line.

Peering in through a door
I jumped out of my skin
and uttered a moan:
bolt upright at a desk,
the ghost of me
staring at my headstone.

ROV's – Remotely Operated Vehicles.
Demons & Diablos are types of vehicle

Firing Squad

The brightest spark in the company
hit on a slick solution to that messy
and distasteful business of redundancy.

At ten one morning the fire alarm sounded.
The workforce duly left their positions
to gather in groups at the fire drill stations.

Inside, management squads deployed
to visit the office of each on their list
and leave a note of regret on the desk.

Returning from muster, the targets,
to their alarm, found they'd been fired,
fifty employees were given the bullet.

They were back in the car park inside an hour,
their contracts in shreds, along with their futures.
The managers hid in their ivory bunkers.

The Captains of Industry do the hiring.
In wartime the cowards get shot.
Now the cowards do the firing.

The Marginal Fields

The bottom's dropped
out of the Barrel again,
and the gravy train
has been derailed
at Aberdeen.

It's the downside
of the fossil fuel boom,
the five-year lull
when all the graphs
plunge off the page.

The Rigs are built
to stand the Hundred
Year Wave: the surfer's
wet wet dream.

But mortgages sink
faster than gangsters
in concrete Reeboks,
and here's me mid-pool,
no snorkel in sight.

I've taken my leave
of e-mail, Autocad,
bosses and tossers
who think
everyone else
is a wanker.

So its back to
the Doledrums;
the Onshore
Survival Course:
stopped cheques,
coffee mornings
with the bailiffs,
Valentines from the
Procurator Fiscal,
Sheriff's Officers
and the Hydro
heavy gang.

I'm holding the fort
until the markets
are buoyant
and the Marginal Fields
surrender their yield.

Meanwhile, I've decided
on the Writer's life:
I'm translating Yevtushenko
into Doric and selling
the texts at reserve
games at Pittodrie.

It's the job
security that
attracts me.

The Sea at Night, Dunbar

Is a notional, unearthly place,
a dreamed room
with no sound ground between
what's seen and what's assumed.

Gannets skim a cliff of air,
the press of spent typhoons.
And round the headland, in the Firth,
the Bass Rock booms.

www.coma

I logged on
as *Global Villager*,
spent hours in
an on-line chat group
really connected
with people
from all over
the world.

Energised,
I went to the pub
but left early
to avoid
my fuckin'
neighbours.

Memorial

Piper
Chanter
Deveron
The bleak black oil is dearly won.

Alpha
Beta
Epsilon
The orange-suited men are gone.

Mark
Matthew
Luke
John
The list goes on, the list goes on.

Arthur
Terry
Kevin
Ron
Their names are gilded by the sun.

Tyne
Mersey
Thames
Don
Their sons now share a common home.

Welder
Diver
Motorman
The love that fuelled their hearts lives on.

FROM THE UNDERGROUND

Epitaph for Nico

The first
Velvet
Under
Ground

Black as Jazz

Let's slip into our shadow-selves again,
and haunt the umber hours until dawn.
We'll seek the hidden raptures down below
the neon-painted pavements of this town.

We'll slide into some room where tunes will plumb
the dark delights of freeform jazz and soul.
And in those minutes we will be alive
to rhythms from a deeper inner tide.

Our skins will turn to mottled midnight tones,
like moonlit snow dissolving over coals.
And should the music bind us to its time,
we'll trade these truant moments for our days.

To live beyond this world where white hours pass:
the continent of night is black as jazz.

Killing Time

I'm drinking alone, and living dangerously,
reading poetry in this skinhead teuchter bar.
I'm reading poems by Polish writers, dispatches
from the ghettos: Krakow, Warsaw; 1944.

It looks as if I'm killing time but I'm really
reconstructing it, fifty heartbeats to a page.

There's been a lack of crack all evening.
The barmaid's just attained the 7th level of boredom.
This Caffrey's is cloudy but it's clearing slowly.
The Lottery Draw's on the Videoscreen.

But my mind's on the book and the scenes it describes:
smoke, gunfire, bombs; the heart's alarms.

The barmaid's eyes are as dull as the decor.
A punter takes a shine to her but gets rebuffed.
Just as well, he slurs, *the only thing that's hard
these days is my luck.*

A Prince among men is wailing from the jukebox:
Tonight I'm gonna party like it's 1999.

It's a song on the end of an epoch.
And there's a song on the end of the world
in the city of Warsaw beneath my thumb, where
a man is writing a book in the ruins of his local pub.

The decor here is frost and swastikas.
The barmaid's shoes are buried in snow.

The man is alone in the smoke and the shadows.
Downing his dregs, he closes the book
on himself. He takes his leave of no-one.
He enters the night. The night enters him.

Jam & Weetabix

Once or twice upon a time,
their next-door neighbours made them breakfast.
One on Mondays, Wednesdays, Fridays.
One each morning in between.
Mum and Dad were out at work
long before the sheets were parted.
Long before his naked body
lay before his aunty's gaze.
He was ten and she was twenty.
He knew she was twice his age.
He knew she was going to hurt him,
like she did each day for years.
She'd done it through his muffled cries,
through his exams and through his tears.
And she rubbed till he was crying.
And she nearly stopped him breathing.
Then she kissed him on the lips,
as you would a willing lover.
And he never told his Dad
and he never told his Mother.
Kept it secret. Held it in.
A first instalment on his cancer.
They would sit, he and his brother,
in the Dachau of their childhood:
their internment in the kitchen,
where their darling next-door neighbours
fed them jam and Weetabix.
And his aunty's anger lingered
through the bleak Assembly sermon;
lingered like a ghost through English,
haunted him through History.

And his pain was never uttered.
And he always felt bewildered,
felt betrayed, maligned, marooned.
His bed adrift on seas of sweat
with his aunty at the helm.
And she gave him cards at Christmas.
And she took him to the circus.
Sat him down and served him breakfast.
Fed him jam and Weetabix.
Smiled when once he spilled his milk.

Bloke

When the work dried up I took to drink.
I pissed my family down the sink.
I left my wife, or she left me,
The kids survive on charity.

It's one for the pain and two for the road.
I'm shifting shit by the lorryload.
I trowel it up and I dish it out:
once with my fists and twice with my mouth.

I hail a cab with a one pound note
and ride until the meter's broke.
The taxi driver wins the chase
and takes his fare out of my face.

Now it's cold on the road at two o'clock.
There's blood on the ice where I took my knocks.
I'm down on my luck and down on me knees,
The snow in my shoes is starting to freeze.

I crawl to the door and stab at the lock.
My hands are frozen into blocks.
I'm dumb in the heart and numb in the head.
It's a thousand stairs up to my bed.

These nights on the ale and days on the dole
soak through your skin and sink your soul.
Fags and whisky make me choke.
I'm broke as a bloke with a hole in his coat.

When the work dried up I took to drink.
I pissed my money down the sink.
My suicide's such a lazy crime:
I'm drowning myself one glass at a time.

In the Offing

Standing like an amputee
with a hundred limbs lopped off,
my neighbours poor denuded tree,
its branches now the chopper's crop.

Now the chainsaw hacks the trunk,
whirring in its brutish cough.
The pinetree teeters like a drunk
then, to meet its shadow, drops.

I sometimes wake in sweat and fright
from scenes and sounds as I nod off.
The chopping barks out every night.
The chopping never stops.

Grimericks

i
The folk who lived here, Mrs Foster,
had a nanny but suddenly lost her.
Too sad to stay,
they soon moved away
to 25 Cromwell Street, Gloucester.

ii
Looking surprised and taken aback, he
felt the gore of his face turning tacky
when a shot from the Knoll
shook him like a rag doll
in that limo in Dallas with Jackie.

iii
Then they piled up our clothes in the snow,
and the children lined up in a row.
A surgeon came,
and gave his name:
Wilkommen, Ich bin Doctor Joe.

Elegy xi
(To Peggy from Ted)

In all too fleeting tenderness
did i caress your dear sweet fingers
with such silences as i have known
or in lonely shadowed whisperings
said beside unsleeping streams of night.

Now should i in mercy find my sleep,
serene dreams bathe your frame in dews
of silver light. The white enraptured realms
of your flesh do house my longings
still perpetual and lingering.

Though death has reaped you with its blade
no season will outstrip the cool hauntings
of your lips. Unmade though your being became
none shall stand in place of you
nor close my open hand.

And yet (though time is emptied now of you)
my heart is still petalled as a flower
and is forever falsely opening.
The tower, though steeped in glooms, must surely
be surmountable and love be renewable as Spring.

Though you are in forever i must live in now,
this unplace where my eyes see day as night,
as through a veil, and though another's hand
in mine may lie, i will hold you strongly in my heart.
You who are my light.
You whom love has placed beyond betrayal.

Not Wavering, Nor Drowning

I sometimes envy those believers
in the healing power of holy waters:
those fishers who are fished by blind decree,
who see the sea and think of Gallilee.

In Songs of Praise on Sundays I divine
with dowser eyes the wells of hope in beads
of sweat that sustain a hymnbook's pages;
pools of human salt on *Rock of Ages*.

I see religion in its liquid state,
with each baptiser an emerging wave
of white belief arising from the dark
to offer every drowning soul an Ark.

They walk along the sure line of their faith;
between the shifting states of flesh and soul.
The pulse's sure decline, the end of breathing.
The ebbing flow of life; the pull of heaven.

Daylight Ghosts

What can you do with the dead
but rebuild them in stone,
enthrone their bones,
salt their graves with tears,

die a little with them?

What can you do with the living
who once held your life
in their hearts, with whom
you shone in shared light,
who are now dead to you?

This question marks a shrine.

Haiku for Hussein

Newsflash – War in East!
Tyrant tanks invade Kuwait.
Ruling classes flee . . .

Let the West unite!
Gather for the new Crusades!
(God is Good and White).

Bless America!
Praise Patriotic missiles!
Hawks sharpen their claws . . .

One Tornado's eye
has caught the Sultan's turret
in its laser sights.

Five hundred lives lost
in the bunker inferno:
only Islam mourns.

CNN report
on the Technoholocaust:
ratings explosion!

Shot down in Iraq,
missing pilot's family's prayers
cross the greatest Gulf.

Israel holds firm:
Nettanyahu woos the world
to the thud of scuds.

For the helpless hours,
the hope-starved soldier's wife is
worth her wait in gold.

Thick slick engulfs Gulf.
Blood and oil intermingle:
birds tarred and feathered.

Oilfields set alight.
Thick black war clouds choke Kuwait.
Send for Red Adair!

Invaders vanquished –
Emir of Kuwait restores
normal tyranny . . .

Twice Bereaved

Do I grieve
for you?
I do.

But more:
I grieve
for two;

for you
and the me
I was with you.

Weight : Loss

What is this loss,
this emptying?

It's a hot room
too small for itself,

too large for anything
but a sob.

My pulse thrums.
A world stops.

A new world turns,
one soul shed.

DREAMS & TRAIN SMOKE

How It Will Be

You will think of her
Less and less,
Although you'll think
No less of her.

These thoughts, though few,
Remain the strongest.
What you lose
Stays with you longest.

Gare du Coeur

There's this cool city, see, and there's a train pulling into the station. The train doesn't have a driver. There is only one passenger. That's me. There's only one person on the platform. That's you. There is not a single other soul in the station. The train will stop so that the exact centre of my window lines up with the exact centre of the line of buttons on your new dress. I will sit looking at you for ages. You'll look back at me. It'll be like we're looking at pictures of each other hanging up on the walls of the train. Like we're in an Art Gallery or something. Looking. Just looking. Then one of us will scratch an itch and the other will grin and then we'll both laugh and then I'll know it'll be time to get off my train. As I alight, with my hopes my only luggage, you'll be watching me with your cool furnace eyes which will look like they're about to laugh and about to cry all at the same time. Your hands will be shaking. I'll smell your perfume and remember all those other nights I smelled that fragrance. I'll remember every detail as if it were being projected on a cinema screen; like a movie of ourselves is showing in black and white on the wall behind you. We'll be standing in the station of an Eastern European city in winter. We'll both be wearing furs. Our breath will mimic the steam from the train. A light fog will envelop the scene so that it will be hard to tell if there's anyone but us on the platform. I will speak to you in Russian the Russian word for 'hello'. You will answer with your eyes, which speak all languages and read every sign and know how the world works and how to break hearts. So many hearts! Such drama! And it will be like I've only just met you and like my every lifetime was spent with you and will be spent with you but I don't know this I only feel it. It's a feeling, nothing more. But sometimes feelings are the only real things on the planet, the only things that can be touched with certainty, while rocks and trees and cities and people and countries crumble to dust all around you. The city outside the station has crumbled. The station is the only remaining building. It exists only to house this moment; to frame this frame of our movie, to give a structure to our desires. The station will be the house of our hearts. A page for our poem.

You will touch my hand; a measured gesture, for you know the power of touch.

The power of human electricity. The shock of erotic voltage.

And so, your hand will be cool, as a marble wall is cool.

But your eyes will lance me. Pin me to the moment, as they always do. This is your power.

The feminine power. The power that will place me on trains , on journeys.

A lone traveller through winter nights.

A soldier of the heart called to the Front.

The bearer of his soul's dispatches.

On trains that travel endless tunnels to your eyes, to your eyes, to your eyes.

And I will arrive endlessly in cool cities, in cold stations, on strangely familiar platforms where a familiar stranger will hold out a cool hand and pin me with her eyes to the moment.

To every moment.

The Season in the Room

She's been here again,
all the signs speak of her:
the landscape draped
across the sofa,
the satin petals
cushioned on the chair.

The indent
in the settee
is from her frock.
Her stock-in-trade filigree
has left its shallow signature.
Yes, she has been here.

Tonight, when eyes
are hostage to sleep,
the sound of scissors
will snip the silence.
A threaded flower will bloom
and a season's colours
will seep through her fingers.

Tomorrow, a small
rectangle of Spring
will be hung
on the living room wall.

Man on the Moon

In the street beside The Lemon Tree
a giggle of tipsy tourists stop
abruptly. One of them, a girl
no older than her tongue, raises
an arm and a finger and tickles
the chin of the moon.
HELLO MOON, she purrs.
MOON, HELLO.

On the pavement by the Prince
a drunken pundit tipples
topsy-turvy into a puddle.
He cuddles his liquid pillow
and serenades the face beside him:
HELLO MOON, he croons.
MOON, HELLO.

Soon every strip of neon,
every registration plate,
every sign and signal
up and down the town
is beaming and blaring
and every tongue is twisted
'round the words:
HELLO MOON, they chorus.
MOON, HELLO.

Sick of all this lunacy,
this moonacy, I drive away
to meet my daughter at her work.
My radio queries:

Andy have you heard about this one. . . ?
It's one of her favourites. Hers.
My daughter's. My only daughter's.

And me, her only father. I have no son.
I have a moon. My own moon.
I orbit her, she orbits me.
What we share is light-
heartedness and the sure and certain
belief that REM will save the world.

This no sooner thought than she's there,
stood stock-still in front of me.
Wide-eyed, mouth agape. Moonstruck.
Her tongue rises above the white horizon
of her teeth:
HELLO MOON, she murmurs,
MOON, HELLO.

Aeons later she disentrances
and I come to her senses:

Thanks for waiting, Dad, and did
you see the moon tonight?
And Dad, did you say
HELLO?

Portrait of Ana Dali

Ana Dali, Salvador's sister,
shown here in an ominous frock,
eloped with an amorous easel
to the melting apartment block.
She waves through a hole in a mirror
sewn into her brother's smock.
As she drinks the breeze from the Pyrenees
Time drips from the village clock.

Her pigtails stretch from her window
to Cadaques and the port of Bilbao.
Over sun-speltered Andalucia
through measureless meadows of cows.
Her lemonade has developed amnesia.
Her maraccas engage in a row.
Her Mercedes Benz is ablaze at both ends.
She is wearing a watch that says NOW!

An orangepeel twist forms her fingers,
her mouth is a door left ajar.
The Atlantic cascades from her shoulders
where Cervantes tilts at the stars.
Her nose is the shape of the town of Cadiz.
Her cheeks form the base of a vase.
Her hair is coiffured in a whirlwind of birds.
Her eyes are Flamenco guitars.

Acrylic skies frame her figure,
painted with luminous grace.
She gazes at astral horizons
in the infinite sadness of space.
She sits in a gilded garden,
a paranoid, marigold place.
She is humming a tune to the Catalan moon
through a veil of vermilion lace.

Love Jazz

Love's a 'bone
And love's a horn
Love is music being born

Love's a horn
and love's a 'bone
Love's a tune
on a saxophone

Oh love is blow
and love is
suck
Pucker
           pucker
    pucker
                    puck

Love is lip jazz
    hip jazz
thigh jazz
Love is lucious
Eye-to-eye
jazz

Love's a drum
And love's a snare
Love's a holiday from care

Be my baby
be my band
be the keyboard
for my hands

When I'm upright
Baby you'll be grand

Out of Dates

40
goes to
the Co-op
Pulls out
a packet
labelled
LOVE

(He'd forgotten
the flavours:
pure & tender /
raw & flirty)

He sighs
and shelves it

The label reads:

Best before
30

Stuff Pythagoras

The affair that is hot news
Is equal to the fun of the affairs
With the other two guys

He said
Obtusely

But this is one triangle
That won't be eternal –
It's a sine of the times

She replied
As she flew off at a tangent

Strange Things, Trains

I got on at Montrose
and sat next to the Pope
and his wife, who were
on vacation from the Vatican.

They were short
on conversation
but were polite
in a Polish sort of way.

He polished his golf clubs
while she polished off
the After Lent Mints.

He asked if I liked his
Reservoir Bhoys
T-shirt, which I did.

Kyrie eleison! Henrik Larsson.
he muttered mysteriously,
then: *Gould, Corr, Kharine – The Goalie Trinity,*
and: *Moravcik crosses better than me!*
He seemed to find this amusing
and he chuckled to Dundee.

As they alighted for St. Andrews
he blessed me twice
for sneezing.

Then a Rangers fan got on:

*Fuck me, was that the Pope
that I just passed?*
He enquired.

That is a correct assumption.
I replied.

Bloody strange things, trains!
He said.

I nodded in confirmation.

The Gap

'Here's where old Gibbons jumped from, Robinson'.
Weldon Kees *Aspects of Robinson*

Robinson at the scene. The bridge. The span. The vertical
drop. A fall from gracelessness, evidently. Robinson musing
over personal items: a wallet, a watch, a ring, a Visa. Neatly
piled at the point of departure. The view from the edge: a breath
taking vista. Metres of air. Fathoms of water. The gap: at a push
the depth of ten buses turned on their noses. He stepped off
the wagon and into the drink, his brinkmanship trumped. A slip
of the tongue twisting fail into fall? Or jilt into jump? A tug,
a dredger churning the bottom. Robinson lobbing a stone overboard
and clocking the time when the stone takes a soaking. The gutting
shed stench cutting into his nostrils. Nauseous odours of petrol
and diesel swim up from the river. Robinson, clueless, turns
up his collar and turns on his heels to track down a diner.
A burger, a Jack, a slim panatella to bridge the gap and fuel the enigma.

I Look Up

A sudden gust flusters
the leaves of the book.
I look up from the poem.
The room has changed.
You are in it.

Your face is the same
as when I last saw it,
though now obscured
by another man's shadow.

Your voice chimes softly
down the years
and whispers past me
on to other rooms.

Always the traveller,
you were just a tourist
in my heart,
collecting souvenirs
for your Love Affair
Museum.

A wet-dream dealer
in stillettos and rouge,
always flirting with mirrors
and smiling at strangers.

I picture you with others,
at airports,
planes lifting all around you.

Sometimes I see you
in slippers, at stoves;
a bedsit refugee,
letterless and lonely.

A sudden gust flusters
the leaves of the book.

I look down at the page.
The poem has changed.
You are in it.